C0-DAM-476

SYMMETRY

Also by Laura Moriarty:

Two Cross Seizings

Persia

Duse

like roads

Rondeaux

L'Archiviste

SYMMETRY

LAURA MORIARTY

AVEC BOOKS
PENNGROVE

Grateful acknowledgment is made to the editors of the following publications in which some of these poems previously appeared: *AVEC, Black Warrior Review, Notus, O/two* anthology and *The Wallace Alexander Gerbode Foundation Awards in Poetry* anthology.

ISBN:1-880713-04-7
Library of Congress Catalogue
Card Number: 95-77361

Cover photograph by Laura Moriarty

©1996 by Laura Moriarty

First Edition

All Rights Reserved.

This book was published in part by generous grants from The Fund For Poetry and The California Arts Council, a state agency.

Avec Books
P.O. Box 1059
Penngrove, CA 94951

FOR NORMA COLE

The right and the left are obtained by letting trail behind you a tinge of *persistence in the situation.* This symmetrical fashioning of the *situation distributed* on each side of the vertical axis is of practical value (as right different from left) only as a residue of experiences on fixed exterior points.

—Marcel Duchamp
from *The Green Box*

THE MUSE

The familiar paraphernalia

Forced into the role of silent collaborator

The psyche at stake

We are in business together

The buildings melt into the sky

You sing to distract me

Your reason is not mine

Is mine

CAPRICE

three four time   Caprice was now a crime

cameo   And if I did, what then?

of bone   On books and boxes, jars

the stenciled   Appearance of the stars

limitless   During the talk

morning   He spelled he explained

illusion   He is not mine

example   The idea of revival

CLEMENTINA

I take pictures of empty streets

We had unlimited refills. At other times he walked by screaming. Other people from there have died. But I still see him

Another form occurs during the wedding march. The narrowness of the path.

The figures in the pictures look toward each other

He decides to take heaven by storm

Alley (he says)

The above is a definition

THE GARDEN

An army massed on the border
A hat on my head
Keeps the sun from my eyes
More than one border is involved
Filled with light

And heat and water
And coffee again paradise
With quiet prepared
Mask at my side or your side

You are on my side
With time to write or
I have a shelter a sealed

Man rests by his mask
The world is thick above and around him

No time

THE BIRTH OF VENUS

As a rosary
As a crucifix
She recreates the senses
Is held

coarse	vast	cast	station
stand		livery	emblem
sewn	start	laid	
bright	case	brine	stet

Eve writes a letter
Grief she says forget me
In waves beaded with foam
It falls over her dress

STORY WITHIN A STORY

One falling figure is the fall through the literal world, the other, the fall by false interpretation

The color of the hailstones is red, white and blue

Numen the gypsy said or sap

Only one who has sinned can be redeemed

and want for want of a better word

This angel is blindfolded

The Rose Parade in Pasadena. That is what we have to look forward to

That and the war

THE SNAKE AND THE NIPPLE

The tea is tangled like an aquarium

"Her eyes hold the tragic past; the formal elements of the painting predict the future."

What is music an example of?

I wish I could get in touch with you by listening to a song but not always the same song

THE SAME SONG

A bird rests behind a vase

The technician sings as she works

Her hair is the color of her skin

An apple made of marble

The horn plays her part

A miniature tree

A copper pot

I spoke to him in the old language she admitted Referring to the one playing the part of the gardener It was like a cipher The reply She called us harebrained But we were the ideas The alternate story was the one in the pictures The same one And positions also similar An impossible openness

AN ENGLISH DREAM

green	ties	head	steam	bell
slant	kneel	stance	blue	leaflet
vine	devious	red	lean	pedestal
roof	path	bush	brick	brazen
post	night	stick	yellow	colophon

LA RUOTA

Fortune is shown in her most common form. Dreaming of rain

The words exist in the original language

She is attached to a wheel

Being entirely transformed into the act of turning

Like taste left in the mouth

She signs her name with her hands

Helpless as gravity

Finding irresistible force the object

Fortune is naked

Retrieved from a status not unlike

Any other tied thing

Or escapes like breath from the head or changes air into water or fire

And back again

A thing inside another thing There is no repetition

And yet more common than desire is

Fortune captured

THE NEW DANCE

I dream of the membrane that separates me from the past

Going backward and forward like a heart machine

Everyone says it for you

And yet there is more physicality

A catalogue is made which reads like a story

A western version symmetrical like a shield

There is a map of the dance included

The contraption does the rest

THAT EXPLODE TOGETHER

It gets worse It gets better
The words seem to shrink
He writes about his experience
I write about mine
Song lyrics on her lips
Make the same sound
The automatic movements were the ones
Isolated like notes
I tell everything in plain words
Thinking against the action
The body changes what is said
I also write in zeroes
The flexibility is exact
He reads as if the words were his
He treats the book like an accordion
She belongs to El Diablo he sings
Over and over they agree
He tears it apart a capella
Her nerves are numbered like stars
Too distant to record

may have replaced the missing cardinal virtue of prudence

He carried an hourglass instead of a lantern. This mistake dates back to the fifteenth century when a woman put an hourglass by her bed and stopped her caresses when it ran out.

There is no difference between that man and his background

He reads like a woman

A card one side flowers
I never doubted that
There is no memory like the past
Held in the hand
The 'pole' star and the 'guard' stars
A table for the new moones
The surveyor makes notes with an assistant
He turns them into a map
The word navigator the translation
The word help alone
A card tells the story on both sides
I can't hide it claims
My attention is yours
Familiar friendly foreign near
It's not only women who disappear
The world unfolds and closes back
Something taken by chance
A card any one

THE ENCHANTER

The Enchanter, pendant to the Adventuress
Identified himself in the landscape taken
From life and from fantasy But can I
Go along with it I thought the court poet
was to the courtesan as the thief to the carriage
The fortune teller's explanation was inevitable
Setting out for the ball and the return from the ball
A standing man dressed in red
Said with all that this entails Let us assemble
Finally an almost invisible statue in the distance
Consists of greenery against which a woman holds
A paper written on her lap
Someone who plays an instrument appears to be
A different size or the scale is different
The trees are too soft like flowers
Something melts something undergoes restoration
He rides inside

ELABORATION

		stag	
pant	flute	stoop	tent
flower	string	flag	slat
cup	lip		fist
last			stem
rain	rest	red	sift
			soft

THE MISSILE

The protected zone
Like a diagram of a pine cone
Removed from life
Lightning
Seems alive

The quiet voice
The trees of an imaginary paradise
Dropping down

Or not fallen
Like people who are innocent
To the ground

To the air or back down
What lasts is what we have

What we have done

You pull me
To you I am
What can be
Unsaid
In a speech
What can this be
That sounds
Hard before
You pull me
Think you say
Nothing later
Or something shaped
So that it changes
The same way
You pull me

The confusion of the angel with the virtue of temperance.
Pouring one thing into the other. Hopelessly mixing
stories. There are separate days but they are also strung
together. You have a magnetic personality she explained.
He wore the red mask of the sun. But he wore it badly.
The black wings were supposed to be gold. The clouds
were made of oil. Other angels presided. Trees grew
under them. Red came in at the bottom under the clear
green. Strength was represented by a man with a cat in a
blue coat. He had an unusual sense of the past. The horses
were white. The cast was upside down. The things inside
pouring out.

We wouldn't be adversaries
If you weren't on my side
Opponent I am not
Unsure of my position
A technicality noted
Is not a complaint
Is what was said
What was written
We wouldn't be admitted
As an entity
We who are not visible
To either one of us
It is an argument that we are
If only we believed now what we knew then
We wouldn't be wrong

Reading a history of madness I feel confused by time. When I write to you you don't write back and then you do and I don't reply. I make you forget my writing. The cases occur during the day. During the night there is nothing. Your book arrives in the mail. The history is there like a letter from my banker. She writes about the things that everyone knows. You complain about me. Those were the sweet times. Or the banker is in cahoots with the future. It's all part of a huge deal. Depth perception suddenly absent. The negotiations are both strident and unspoken. I look up from my book as if I'd heard a voice. There were days when you could be exposed with honor. The madness is that they are over.

Things change until they don't exist. Evolution is not improvement. These pictures of time look like today. I tell people about you. And they were from only one journey. "For the stranger of our time exploration is impossible." And am not believed.

The leafy tangerines are the lucky ones. A stern example of excess. An hourglass with many chambers and an unlimited supply of sand. A woman's breast. Is that what you imagined? Or is this more like it?

THE PROCURESS

If you cause me to act
By your most intimate will
You put your hand on the breast
Of the procuress red
As if through a lens
Sharpens the senses
The subject in relief
Handmade lace gold coin thick
Glass again seen through completely
Is this account without meaning
To remain you turn back
To look over your shoulder at nothing
Or at darkness pictured
The places covered with linen
Again we begin
If you cause me
To act on your behalf
A verbal contract in other words
Not valid but accurate
A feminine form imagined
To consist of penstrokes instead
Of flesh we speak of her
In the third person
As if there were a difference
Between us the obvious one
Of being what we are
Not able to see
That this is all it is
Statement and persuasion
An analysis of the physical aspects

Of sight speaking candidly
The desirable things
Their antitheses
Love itself embodied perspective
Flattened out into a map
If you cause me to act

PHYSICS

The bowl of fruit makes its own sun. We leave our maps behind and get into the pure distance. People tell us what we want to know. There are armies of thieves. The thing they want most. The radio is like being present. Simultaneously one sleeps. One reads a letter. The world is folded. The afternoon is almost over. Yellow apples fall onto a rug. Repetition is implied in the way things bend. We respond to the natural laws. We are lost. A tent on the plateau. Nothing to stop the wind. The bowl in slow motion appears to pour. The woman to hold the letter steady.

We get to the point of only reflected light. Your glasses ache on your face. You stare at the way roses put shadows on a vase. A drawing is made of tar, masonite and plaster. They are called black roses but they are red. Made of tile with the minerals baked in. One after the other like the white spots on dominoes. There is a reversal. She is a physicist. Her numbers represent events. Your eyes at rest in your head. Your words in your throat.

WHAT IS SAID

Their words can be used against them
They are faithful and confident
We are them in their sense
In ours we dance to a slow song
One example of a solution is strength
Or in numbers
Where we are multiple
The story is said to unfold
Their words to be said again
By others pretending to be us
But they are men/women and we are women/men
It's like another planet
Or like people who don't see themselves
Though they stand before each other
Their words said

What is claimed
A companion piece to what is said
If I had to put it all on red
Or on black I would be a gambler
And this would be my story
But I am not that
Object if you will or if not
This is not a practice hand
What is claimed
Is that chance exists
Spinning us in or out
Time is on the side it's always on
Like a bracelet like the physical
Hand it surrounds
What is claimed

DISCOURSE

Formulations of this sort are perhaps unduly stimulating

Civilization is an action of course transitive necessarily energy comes from the destruction of something someone

Somewhere around the year 1100, we come upon the first vernacular love poetry in a modern tongue. Its form is novel, its provenance uncertain, its substance strange. Everything about it is mysterious. (Maurice Valency, *In Praise of Love,* 1961)

As playing cards are first mentioned in a law forbidding gambling, love is said to have been codified by Andreas Capellanus in what to us seems clearly a satire. Indeed what could be more absurd?

Be brave and remember me
To believe in a construction
To have believed entirely
Against the rational
Is only as good
As the last moment
Made of possibility
Or if not
Be brave for nothing
Is the only honor
Worth the hour having gone
Away as always the same
Or only sounds
Accumulate as if they could
Be brave without us

The honey

Making tea again spring

The honey loose

THE FACTS

Don't answer any questions

A quick dry and a slow drying surface

A dream about action a reverie

About face the sense of being saved

I'm in a drought and it rains

The two times coincide

One doesn't end one does

MINIATURE

The manuscript suggests an allover approach to life. Instead of sky there is design. There is a consistent relationship with perspective. There is no use for it. The designs represent each other. A tree is about to become part of a seamless landscape. The background is pure. It repeats. It is blue but has no more reality than the formula for oxygen. The tree doesn't either. It was a thousand years ago but nothing has changed. You don't hear my voice when I write. I don't hear yours when you read. Representation of the body does not occur but the subject is obvious. The tree doesn't fall. Algebra is invented and then lost. Chemistry.

WE SEE

Twilight
Weather bad
Or here warming warning
Spring can't be
Dangerous this fast

The past mistaken
For what happened
An unimaginable scene
Accompanied by a jackal

This figure also not
Known not said
Blind sight when you

See what you can't see
Illusion or change

You can't know

SONG

There is a song
About repetition
There is a red sun
Incoming like a siren
Or the steady

All clear all wrong
That we see each other
Flatly
Long range

Life as in taking too much
Describes the weapons
The words blood

Friendly the boys
Among them fire

Us

Any change is revenge
Improvement illusion
The same as actual improvement
I am free
To say anything
The ultimate manipulation
Is the truth suddenly taken
We agree to pretend
Nothing that happens
Has to do with our agreement
To disagree as if we were colleagues
In a grand endeavor which we are
Known completely to each other
However invisible

THE PARADISE OF DAINTY DEVICES

Every word every sound
A book of alternating moons and suns
Nothing is effective as a strategy
But exhausting and expensive

It's all that gold
In my head musical
Fragments a statement
For a song

To be only that
Which like seasons
It isn't always winter
Or the title a question

A commentary
Nothing is wrong
The original just didn't get that far
That fast or did

I would like to complain
She says about you
The gold was the sun
The moon nothing

WE MEET

The chalice of the atmosphere
A cross-hatching of light
An armored glass
A failed but ancient
Experiment which fails again

Live by definition
What actually
Or by machine
An old manifestation

Happens at any time
You see it
Simultaneously

We aren't the same
The way they see us

Looking back at them

ROCOCO

The circular

Photograph of a fragment of the solar halo
In the halo book I represent you
Like an autograph
I give it away
Definition by definition

Memory is light
Meaning brighter
The pattern comes from the world
We anticipate

The curves before we see them
We know what they are
What they are saying

Angels suggested
Saints praised

The triumph of nature over nature

WE DECIDE

Ahead of time
Gone to those lengths
Known only
Like travellers arrive
Hat in hand

Any time
Anywhere

I

WE WERE

When it started
When it ended
We were there
We are uncontrollable
In our passions

The war is everything
Goes on as before
The air in my head
Is the same air

Used as thought or shot
Or song repeated
Doesn't end

We are persuaded we hear princes soldiers women
On the air fire metal water men darkness

We are there again

NO CLOSURE

The window breaks down
Stunned and surrounded
There is no horizon
Where I am
Not less

Breath not breath
Stay
With no reason
Than here

It begins it began
The same "projecting
the transient closure of a casual gaze

into a concentrated field
of divine fixation."

But what is an image?

BALLAD

Dance with this one
Sing with that one
The results are blatant
Abrupt and baffling

Wipe the sleep from your eyes
He tells me
Nothing is happening in the war
They are stuck closed

It's the principle of the thing
I know the instrumentation
"Only too damn bloody well"
He joins the band
They march all over hell

THERE IS NO

Lack of harmony

Between form and meaning

Symmetry

THE NAME OF

The helpless similarity
Sleep in fury
"Messalina in pursuit of the god"
Who does not exist
Who knows

About me
The walls survive
Snipers surrender
I do

As an allegory
What I was looking for
Exhausted

Hopeless
These are my terms

My love

SLAVE

You are a messenger my friend
And so deserve no blame
The cruel transformation
I had to find my hunger
Into Dulcinea
Coming back
May I have the honor of
The mistress of thought
And bring it intact
If I were
Only

DULCINEA

But words aren't equal to anything

Any change

I hate I love

This place damn it

An absence which repeats itself while we are occupied
with fierce attention

The relief of being enough

Your face frames your eyes with a new roughness
which gets rougher every day I read

an enormous book to keep from thinking but I think
while I read I take outlandish pleasure in the narrative.
The relief is physical

The pleasure random

THE MOUTH

We have words
Over definition
Terror
Something to lose
Loose
In us
Harshness
Oracularity

A stone bath or wood room vivid and liquid ritual means
the wished for repetition against the sense of what is said
at the same time taking in the heart the belly the groin the
mouth and legs the ass the chest and eyes.

THE LAW

Those of us
Without the future
Or throughout
These pearls for eyes
These teeth
He gave his love a white clock

THE SONG IS FOR SALE

You can see my body
Reread

Empty lake shape
In whatever measure

I am strong
I am not strong

A solid becomes a void (a mountain
disappears a structure burns)

The sequence is known

ASTROLOGY

A monk is viciously on the phone. It's a costume. I recognize no one. A red devil hovers over the table . . . elliptical shapes threaten to explode or release in some fashion. We can say anything. We are charged. Things get out of hand. Another interpretation. An allegorical still life. I read about the sun knowing it's the moon I should read. The stars.

STOP

Gold bell
Red mill

Now this question of sovereignty
And of illusion
Better speak

"Sovereignty is NOTHING"

A restatement

A gift seen as an explosion
With no context

Needed quiet
Hunger

The city where we

THE DOUBLE

I can't wait
Speak
Know

Screamed apparently again
Woke

Not awake
No

VALÁSQUEZ

He is a devil
I remind myself
I have you on my hands
Here you are

Like flowers
Tea stains the cup
I take it that way now
Too strong

Devils collect
At the edge of the ceiling
The black Helen
In the Spanish heaven

His gold
Yours
You
Not you

VENUS PRONE

"The ends of heaven like a Garment will I fold them
around me" (William Blake)

Or take your picture

Your part

Elongated

Before in profile and after

Being them or each other. Laughter with complicity
with character. Let's pretend. Let's take advantage of
their confusion. We are real.

Elongated the planes of the body you have the colored
shadows of your waist. A baby holds the mirror up.
You look rested. Baby. Framed. Taken.

I have wrested the frame from him.

The ache from you

Is my own

The meter running
While we speak
Calculates an equal
Silent figure known
To us adds to our sense
Of what is not
Impossible
To betray by speech alone
The meter the figure knows
Speech is free or almost
Free because it is not
The cost is written even
Spoken forever is owned
By each one who knows
The meter is told

TEA

Painted sky

Glass with vines wound

Hell or heaven also painted

Or silver lemon peeled

Overturned the top open

To the world

Shells plates pale

Cloth napkins cream

Paper

There is no place
I can go
That you won't
Know understand figure follow hold as I hold
You

Use the word
As a name
As I did
I do

But you knew that
We are blind
I am senseless

And the opposite is true
There is no time

We don't go on

DOLORES

Drunk again
Rain locally
Of a woman with life
In my arms

I am in love with a painting
Taste
Unwilling
Pain

Vigilant
Cause of our joy
Enough
Lady

She is one
Angry
Christ
After the flagellation

Before dawn
Overstated
Babylon
 Chaste

Canaan
Just far
Painted
Our

ANTIDISESTABLISHMENTARIANISM

You have control
You get used to it
Warned
Useless
Know this

The longer the word the longer
You hold your breath you
Said you were right I lost
There is no warning

Possible
To say nothing ends
Without saying again

The world
Without knowing

You have

TARANTULA

Not pride but fear. The personifications were lost. It was
a conversation we had been having for some time. The
allegory was stiff inside of us. We cried differently. As if
we were the dangerous ones. It was your story being told
by me. Music strangely slowed. The exhausted chorus.
Virtues half-dressed smoking in the corner.

AKASHIC RECORDS

On the Revolutions of Heavenly Bodies

The presence in the universe of observation

Copernicus returns and we share him

Questions of magnification. We rent a camera and
then a planetarium. We hire swans and a stenographer.
Here we are at the zoo.

A hotel room. A court reporter.

A series of them

The writing uncovered

ASTRONOMY

He looks to me
To see of you
What reflection
Makes the moon
In this system am I

The same lined
Precision the same
Silence
You say he is

Or he says there is no history
To someone else or science
I say nothing

The world writing the moon
Is the distance between them and you

Between us

Be good
I think
To him
Accept this
As what it is
Nothing exists
As simply
Could or can't
Be good
To us
As our words
Or word given to you
You to him
Only can
Be good

SPEAK

Jealous virgin	Unbruised
Forget the padlock on this closed	
Fragrant store	Tin
Forget the orange	Forms
Especially	Birds
Too bright stones	Eaten by
Clear	Calling
Bad liquor	Chocolate
Sky fallen	Child
Cake sugary flat as the plain	
Ask nothing	Nothing
Gained	Dissolves
Or tart	The lime
Takes and triangular	Skin
Cup cold	Tongue

MEMORY

I pull the earphones around me like a blanket the cord
transmits the future into my mind. A man with a saint's
name. A robe full of thorns. I pull from my chest and
arms. One at a time. And eyes. More about them. Less
you. A shawl knitted into the wire. They read the same.
The lids are like masks of your face. It's a circus routine.
A clown song. A woman tied to a chair does nothing.
Monkeys. Tigers. Swans.

READING

The one clear night which encompasses the subject
forgets everything. Everyone in a situation is indirect.
The stupid one is lucky. The beautiful angry. The absent
wise. You transparent I. The subject wakes further.
Queasy with brightness. Tightly waiting but open.
Open.

SONG

The mistake would have been audible to only one person. But I was that one. The musical version you preferred played. The question became double. If a statement had occurred at that point anyone would have waited. Though if not not. No one could have known what was wanted. Least of all oneself. The distancing mechanisms were the naked ones. There were no words.

NIGHT 1

A foreign waltz predicts my future. Interrupted or off-key and then resolved back into an hypnotically familiar rhythm. As if thoughtful pausing. Falling. Landscapes considered and rejected. Without thought. As too wet or too green. Or too bright.

I see myself in the reader's dream also as the subject of forgetting. A skeptic has no trouble explaining this. But the writer doesn't see him. I can't sleep. He claims. Haven't slept. Not dreaming was the punishment. The steps in the waltz took us back. "The dream ends" is an end to the poem in a visual sense only.

As in repossessed. Iron bands also from the poem take the place of bones producing a heaviness not unlike sleep. A work written by hand over and over. The tea is a potion. The waltz is foreign but intelligible. This is the last of the false mornings. The words rinsed into the cup. Bones played. Note for note.

It is the same waltz. They are the bones. Sleep has been eliminated. The backdrops depict the middle of the day. Not like the one we are in pouring. But an imaginary place. Italy. Like the scrapbook. The pictures on my forehead.

NIGHT 2

Translation is a metaphor for nothing. Nothing changes. The struggle is overcome by giving in. The rain is light but steady. There is no such thing as pain in that language. You must say something else. One can rest into the knowledge of what doesn't happen being like what does. It is being written at the same time as the poem. The letter. The moon.

". . . at that sight blushed scarlet red,/The stars threw down their cups and fled. . . " (William Blake) The moon considered here is the same. ". . . at times explained— which, at bottom, changes nothing." (Georges Bataille, translated by Leslie Anne Boldt) The explanation is unnecessary. I do it purely for your amusement. The tale is told but doesn't solve itself. The issue of forgetting is forgotten. *Carmen* is sung. I picture myself out though I am in. Day through night. It is a conflation of sensibilities. The orientalism of Spain. Gypsies. "Those Egyptians at the edge of town." (*Wolf Man Meets Frankenstein*) Lon Chaney takes over with his pathos. His desire to escape from the animal within. From the moon.

NIGHT 3

The ability to sit still for a thousand hours. The neon grows more rose. Scheherazade occupies a blue field interrupts the dusk. A clock shows through its filigree. Numbers appear. The cafe is named for a city. People argue over where to eat. I dream this. I am home. Sleepless. A man walks by with flowers wrapped in a Chinese paper. I can't see the words. I can't imagine what they would say if I could see them. There is a flag painted on a post of a vanquished country. I try to sleep hoisting this blank thing. "In the abandon in which I am lost. . ." A writer makes a verb into a country. He claims to be a foreigner in it. The cafe is named for a composer. He is faithless and difficult. His advice is simple. It is music.

NIGHT 4

The essay about sacred and profane laughter was not good as a soporific. And the artist was German. She has kept me up for days with her two-headed women and trompe l'oeil. A man passes in front of the cafe. He is soaked. It's almost dark. He has a white cane. A woman squats in the rain pissing between cars. (This is later and far away in another country.) Sleeping and not sleeping begin to seem more alike. She is drunk. There is blue around her eyes like paint. Too dark and bright for the situation which is casual. But the shadows in this illusion are really cast. The storm breaks up. It's another time again entirely.

NIGHT 5

The sleep that I pursue is like one of our canceled appointments. Or like the series of them arranged in the calendars we keep emptily. A day of Scotch and chocolate. Vietnamese food. I rent movies and don't see them. We don't meet. I don't sleep but I don't mind. I've gone beyond the need for sleep. Your displacement is the perfect argument for the movies. I heat the coffee forget to drink and heat it again but it gets cold. I bring it to the woman at the espresso machine like an offering. Like a sleepwalker.

NIGHT 6

The night can only happen in this one cafe. Returning here I think of home. Of riced chocolate. Daunting continuity. Opera full blown. Black soot sifts through the house. The roofers sing when it's day. It's not now. Birds fly into the common area at work. Black and yellow eyes. Harsh laughter. The paint peels from the sides like layers of sleep. The roof is taken off. In the house I am awake. The word thing. The capacity is forgotten. The roofers pull out. Thing means singularity. An illusion of wakefulness. Everywhere I go you are. Not sleeping.

A troubled man faces into the wall smoking. This is the future. A lover thinks. Not unlike other stories. Bread for dinner. Bread for breakfast. Insomnia. Lunch. Organization. A woman balances her cup on her saucer. The cafe at the north station doesn't close. An ocean of empty chairs. Pink walls. A family being children together. She is impatient to see him. They come to the cafe in the afternoon. We are headed north. The chairs are woven. The population asleep. At this hour. Broken. Open. Faces onto the platforms. The green trains.

CARMEN

I couldn't speak the new language until I let go of the old one. The old language was like a headache. The new unexpected pleasure. Trouble held my head in place. I remind myself that French and Spanish do not meet in Bizet. There is an absence of Spanish. And yet not. Does absence presuppose a former occupation? Possession? The mind in this case a country, continent, or stage. The body is left. The language we spoke invoked here for example. The last two citizens of Atlantis. Late night science fiction completely mute. The drama is an excuse for what happens to them.

I see someone's lover from a train. He is writing a book without an end. He looks ahead levelly. Floats up the escalator.

A book is rewritten. As I read I feel faithless to the old language but find I don't care what it used to say. Still it is difficult to accept this pleasure. The language is present. Like science it frames the events which get us to the special effects. Voices combine with instruments. Bodies are everywhere. It has been quite an act. We think of the language as secondary to the pain we share which is caused by thoughts of pleasure. There is a hidden author. He moves unreachably through the corridors of the station.

NIGHT 8

The night continues before I have time to think. Incapable of agreeing with the proposition. In the cafe surrounded. But not able to escape. The usual smoke of night. Comes from outside to inside. Stays inside. Flooded as a matter of course in dreams. In other dreams previous to the night in which stranded. The pale linoleum. The pattern known without thought. Is the bottom.

Reached here reading something written in these circumstances. The desire not to sleep. To keep the options open. Open the light. They say in the vernacular of overwhelming fatigue. The reading takes itself to be final. The insomnia is critical. Night as genre or commitment. Writing as time.

We are capable of destroying ourselves. It's almost irre-
sistible. The fire that a man produces. The atmosphere is
consumed. Gifts are forced upon us. They are emblem-
atic of other judgments. The one by water. The one in
which a lion turns into a man and back again. The night
doesn't end but shows through like a jungle. The exploited
sadness of the colonies. We long to go back to the old
country. But have never gone. Sleep is a tale from there.
The end of the world embroidered onto a big silk thing.
Like a cape. Take it from me. I dream. Wakefulness
floods already tangled nerves. Veins stay blue until they
are opened. Nakedness makes it easy to read. The glaring
light of night. A hand is held against me until I am warm.
Tightly like one cupping a breast in Cranach. Or hot like
a horse whose throat the lion takes lovingly in its mouth.

The destruction is in your head. I get stronger as I get
older. But never strong enough. It's that riding in place.
Thick iron weights. But only so long. Takes the place of
white in my bones. Forced awake. Absolutely still. The
cafe livid. The flowers at our table also lit. The flames
painted into the wall. They are real. Desperate to sleep.
Each imagined ending false. The trumpets for example.
The breath for blowing goes back into the mouth. The
thing blown. The ceiling edged with sharp-tailed swal-
lows. They come down on us like people falling. Drunk
with it. They can't hear or see. The sleeping. Overtaken.
We listen for them.

TIME STOPPED SONG

Hand drawn

Red boat   Unassembled

Throat

A man jumps from an animal

With longing with bells

More than enough rope

Hand drawn   Cloak

Those with chance

Why yes Why no

Why not go

It's all talk and talk is bound by oceans

Ahead full Behind time

BUT

Not at the same time
The place not
The eyes are at play
By the book

The room filled with soft cloudy light
The flowers also colorless

In retrospect
Honest during the conversation
Was I

BLOOD

Blood but good
This natural
Letting
Alone go I told
The time again
To myself
On

DAYS AND LIGHTS

Lights pricked out on the blue

Water swept past or poured

Plain in sky at night lit

xerox   horizon   scrap   drum

Green fruit plum moon glory

What astounded saw

Uncertain landscape I

numb   bull   wing   seen

maze   bit   boast   morn

AFTER LAUGHTER

He found the perfect book
Replaced everything I wanted
With ability
Turn around every time I
Go back and

Forth happier
Than ever before
I name a painting
Before laughter

After knowing because
The words fell from his mouth
He held his head in his hand

When I was in it
His head

I read

THE DYING

They lack a segment of their trajectories

The translucent cloth passes from mother to daughter

With gold thread

The light on an edge of street as I write

Has nothing to do with territory

Can't see back

NO STORY

A landscape is disarranged in our time. Water is discontinued. Light. We expect to go on and do. "I remember you" we sing thinking of the war. The motif suggests the judgment we were trained to expect in childhood. The last one.

The bombs have names like Take This or Population Zero. One For Me. One For You. They are signed. Equally missiles and admonitions fill the air. We know the rules by heart but there is no one to give up to.

We mean something difficult to say like absence. We are enforced. Or difficult to repeat. We hope to speak in the future only. The presence of the sun through the fog is morning. When it's spring here it's night there. It's a desert. Whatever else I think I am thinking of you.

There is an antenna on top of the building I have seen but not in person like a claw. Or it is behind my eyes when they are closed. Explosions like letters are silent there. No story is connected to this event which is ongoing. I wish to write directly to someone in another story.

Someone else says it's in the language implying an interest in duplicity. Or that falseness will expose itself. Should it be presented. I don't know why this doesn't seem true. Perhaps because it is understood that there is no value to understanding.

In the distance the antenna is clear like a skeleton. Cards are played. Judgment day after day. "Why not just say it?" we say. And we do. We level blame uninterrupted like a laser. It comes back at us. There is no value to understanding because complicity is authorized. We have it ourselves. We have everything.

People in the democracy movement write poems. They are translated. I wonder about the body of the person writing. There is no question about the accuracy of these words. It is simply absent.

We blow our own horn. There are no supernatural beings to commit these actions. You and I are ordinary. We are left to act accordingly. The city has been ravaged before. We were there to repair it. Where are we now?

A woman is used to not being. A man is a target. Few are coming out. We hope to be one of them. We describe the craters like they were on the moon. The routine of daily life is what we want. The details take over like religion. I want to know all I can stand to know but am not allowed that limit. You are in my mind. I close picturing a human hand. My eyes.

FOREVER

PLUMAS

Flashing jay. Stellar. Wings and body. Sky. Lake. Blue vase. Ultra. Deep night. Stratosphere. Ink.

The roof pale blue. The trees black.

Cloudy though still warm.

A discordant chorus.

Fowl.

Chimera. A fox. Stunned by light.

At dusk a man fishes for trout.

Lamplight. Kimono. Night again.

Day again. Goose quill.

We write.

Down and feathers. Inland beach. We read.

About symmetry about

Sound.

Spoon against cup. Toast.

Surface choppy. Husband. Thought.

People sleep in rented boats.

Geese on the beach. Grass and clover.

There is a storm. The lake is audible. The rain sweeps from the west. Our boat seems.

The memory of something. The waves were gold. I dream I know someone. But there is no point in knowing.

Reading about the city in the country. At night.

The air is filled with the sound of a piper.

Writing.

The city of those thinking of the city.

Up here they are a deep.

Afternoon sleeping. Blue.

The cell receives information in material form.

Time of day. Storm.

Coffee. Notebook.

"The very concept of a form, with an internal self-'reflection' or duplicate of itself as its defining characteristic — the concept, in other words, of symmetry with its constitutive dualisms (reflectional symmetry and rotational symmetry, asymmetry as itself determined by symmetry and so on) — implies a circumscribed space: a body with contours and boundaries."

A book with a sky on it. *The Production of Space.*
Lefebvre.

Or song.

"The casket is empty
Abandon ye all hope
They ran off with the money
And left us with the rope."

The Pogues.

The blue dishes we bring from home.

Goose. Geese.

Leaves among them. A small one with a loud song.

Osprey.

Sleep before diving.

We sleep or walk.

Thick with flowers.

The blue dock.

When we move
The objects have a new arrangement
But are the thoughts
We recognize in them
What "we"
"And as for me" (from a song)
And as for me
Not knowing

Summer seems dark though the days are long. The brightness is flooded with an absence of memory and obsession. There are questions.

Unasked. We get ready to go but don't go.

Questions about possibility.

A single and occasional cloud of butterflies in the heat of the day. Goose down.

Noon and wind.

What we are
When most (unconsciously)
The same is a remembered
Song from a movie of a book
About memory A part
Altered to fit the music
When we play (ourselves)

Cabaret

I have you then.

A jar of wings.

Two clowns in a canoe.

A blackbird shaking the bright body. Black and blue. Yellow.

Left shaking. Wings.

Black and white lake. Night.

My sleeping. Rented.

Seen from a chair in the corner.

Love.

Bucks Lake, Plumas County, May, 1992

RADAR

Late afternoon

In the warm sector of the typhoon

The day in which one has an extra hour

Like an inverted x-ray of the sky

It takes down the trailers and tents, hotels

But they are not symmetrically distributed throughout
the storm

Like stiff white flowers almost invisible against the clouds

Unnoticed the petals curve upward

INSTRUMENTATION

In a blackened room one floor below

His face bathed in a glow

Activity grows like the cloud itself

Astonishment appears like a mask

Before morning

THE CATASTROPHIST

There is no electricity to run the machines in the
hospital

Or to heat or cook

She begins to think of tropical storms

Redfield cyclones can be seen on the wall

She breathes an infinitely small mass of air

The map is in motion

What can be done about the weather or lack of it?

What can the machines tell us?

SCIENCE

Collapsed between two metal cases of books in a pleasantly institutional setting, she felt rested. The carpet made the floor welcome. One of the colors in the case was included in the weave. It was a muted rust. The carpet was thought out. The windows were dark like obsidian, but they seemed to magnify the light.

At the edge of the glass clouds were rising. The flash seemed to come from inside oneself. There was no time for thunder. It was a rare storm. Diagrams were open on her lap. She sat cross-legged, a pile of books in front of her, another precarious at her back. Large pines shook like gigantic wings, wrapped themselves around the building.

THE UNTUNING OF THE SKY

At last we could see through the clouds
With our instruments at the ready
Rain shafts, hail, layers of ice
Snakes coiled inside metal packs

A whole cloud was needed

The sexual aspect of storms
"Horned moon" as holding in the hands
Travels a channel in turn
Blown by

TRIGGERED LIGHTNING

Residents should not be alarmed by oddly shaped clouds

A Faraday cage is an enclosed environment which protects us.

A cloud is an aerosol

An unguent a lacquer

A serpent clawing to get inside or outside.

TRAVNIK

Albategnius, a comet in the sphere of Venus

Travnik, a town

And so it went for a while like a lullaby. "No years wearing them down. . . " or so we believed of the stars. Major Andrew Venus expects the city to fall next week. The people in it are said to have no future. Even at night with no lights the routes of supply are ineffective.

"We are shot but not killed." " We are killed." The sky is compromised. We are gathered at another border, which we believe will be breached, outraged. We are unable to return or cross over.

HECTIC FEVERS

The planetary curve of the sun

Observed from here

A thumbprint on a picture

In a heatwave we feel that the city is an exotic place

We drink tea in spite of the sultriness of the day

This picture of a stationary anticyclone contains only a
mountain and a city, grasslands

Wildflowers

Like a victorious army dancing across the fields

THE DAYS AND NIGHTS
OF THE RAINY SEASON

Find a worthy interlocutor
When the moon is on her back

Like an elephant's tusk stuck
In a painted heaven

Half-visible trees
Prepare to bear fruit

A four-poster room within
A tower of rooms for the wind

We see the flood
In the corner of our attention

A table or island anywhere
We are a landscape saturated

With colors lit
With hands shaken

He responds with a smile
Represented as a curtain

The sun in the sky
As a reptile

Curled in the grass
Among her limbs

PAINTING OF RAIN

Pouring louder
Than the city sounds

Yellow (dreaming of
Yellow) during rain

Scarf stockings
Gloves ancient globe

The creamy ocean
Mapped out against green

And pink masses
Like unexplored

Parts of us Lightning
The inside dark

Room alone
All the colors wet

Our talks unconnected
To this thought of them

Running together (the window)
If we (open)

HOAR AND THIEF

And frost, even slight

"Like a very thin fog that falls softly from the air in which it is suspended"

Matter that could form into dew

What is the source of the cold?

". . . because the fire, adhering to the water, tries to get in from all directions. . ."

"The next step is to see the two phenomena as identical."

3 DAYS

Where wide views of the sky are available

Warm air invades a region

The clouds can be found in the texture of the paper

A thousand miles and three days away

On which they are drawn

Storms for the rest of the continent born

Here if you could only see them

SYZYGY AND BIRTHDAY

A gentle soaking

Warm front travels southward

Or becomes occluded and for days

Larger because closer the moon

Rains to the edge of the sea

Where the sea takes over

The Great Salt Lake, seen from a plane, in the
imagination. Surrounded with salt and snow.

SHOT

As this shot was taken

Dry air in rough country

We are not visible but are present even thriving

A still cloud in which no moisture boils

Where we can see it

The moon is hot

SOME PLUMP

Some plump deity appears
Being honored by garlands
Jostled by winds
Released from houses
Where they are stored

But in our thinking,
Unstored, are free
To combine with elements
Like ourselves
Weight and velocity

As, seated on a tiger,
She pursues
She gives off
Heat or becomes heated
Moving toward

THE LARGE GLASS

The glass is a weather map
A man stands behind
Or through it more or less
He doesn't see the same map but holds
In his mind the one we see
Before him

A destination a woman
Sees herself as that
World crossed isobars
Made of numbers infinitely
Getting larger and smaller
Less than the future

Spontaneity a peppery smell
Carnations with edges. Veins
Give way on the inside. The past
Still attached flowers
Her skin redolent while sleeping
Of moisture

And earth packed
It doesn't matter what happened
The barrels burst
But not during the story
Her section of the glass
His work room

Dying back it's called
Dead Can Dance
An unintelligible waltz
A convention of gardeners
Lust in the Dust
We have nothing in common

She lies
The mud in your mouth is mine
Gifts from the country: fruit
Flowers eggs animals trees fire
She does anything to get you
Anything

To stand in this place
On either side of the glass
The examination
The waiting room
Slow motion forecast
Turn it off

Not having to wait
The spoken life
The man at the gate naked
Like a statue crossed with
A line from a contract
He plays the victim

While giving the weather
I read you
Unput together
The sky at night
Unpredictably silent
Violent speech

There is nothing to say about the weather
Strange on the inside
Funny senseless clown
Mr. Chance looks down on us
Ridges melt outside. Clouds
Sun like honey

DIAGRAM

"*Practice is Art   If you leave off you are Lost*"
—William Blake

For discovery at a future time
A wooden something
Spent the morning writing letters
A spinning air

The western dragon
Weather written on its back it
Is the sky falling
Horned and whiskered

Blake's Laocoön
Waking whispered to me
"I dreamed I was writing. . ."
"Practice is. . ."

Raising his arms in the air
He says everything
Seeing the head through the hair
The printed veins

Paper is an active background
Both of us inside
This preoccupied creature
Painted

To look like good luck
Or like blood
Stays inside or doesn't
This animal

Is a pattern
Legible from above
Looking down at a body
Not in pain

The twister took the walls
Grandmother and child
Anymore
But would rather be

Today in paradise
Can be read from either side
The body doesn't fall away
Or does fall

Into a certain shape
You smile or read in your sleep
You wake up in it
Or partly wake

A common thing
Like breathing
But more ornate
As food also

Stays inside or doesn't stay
Sleeping after the game
Sleeping before the game
A city as if through the air

Repeatedly falls
Asleep during the emergency
The rumpled surface of a person
Quiet now

The grandmother might have said
But the child would have known
There is no such animal
Everywhere

The tail in your hair
And mouth and eyes
Bursts out the walls
People die

Unquietly
Sitting anyway
A creature eats   A saint
emerges hands folded against

A metallic rhythm
Painted on a book
Patroness of how things hold together
And are torn

Face to face with a dragon
Actually a puppet inside
A man inside loose clothing
Wet

For some terrible reason
An exact replica
Of a thing that can't be known
Some mindless storm

Already past
Or went on forever
Only the visibility changing
Or the negotiations

There were no negotiations
You leave or you don't
You can't argue with the weather
The breathing of this animal

Is not compatible with breath
Unless the air of the world
The very thing we want
To include is not included

Which changes the creature
Inside and outside
The sense of the storm, breathing,
Negotiation, death and representing

Impossible as I stand
Or sit waiting for another
Sound to come out recognizable
As life

There is always time
For the whole storm
Is made up like the animal
Startled

Rain late in the season
To do things
Staying inside all of one part
Of one day going on

photo by Nick Robinson

LAURA MORIARTY was born in St. Paul, Minnesota in 1952. Her recent books are *like roads* (Kelsey St. Press), *Rondeaux* (Roof Books) and *L'Archiviste* (Zasterle Press). *Persia* co-won The Poetry Center Book Award in 1983. She received a Wallace Alexander Gerbode Foundation Award in Poetry in 1992. Since 1986 she has been the Archives Director at The Poetry Center and American Poetry Archives at San Francisco State University. She lives in Albany, California.